TEAM SPIRIT®

SMART BOOKS FOR YOUNG FANS

THE INDIANAPOLIS COLTS

BY
MARK STEWART

NORWOODHOUSE PRESS

CHICAGO, ILLINOIS

Norwood House Press
P.O. Box 316598
Chicago, Illinois 60631

For information regarding Norwood House Press, please visit our website at:
www.norwoodhousepress.com or call 866-565-2900.

All photos courtesy of Getty Images except the following:
SportsChrome (4, 12), TCMA, Ltd. (6),
Black Book Partners (8, 10, 11, 14, 19, 25, 26, 27, 29, 35 bottom, 39, 40, 41),
Bowman Gum Co. (15, 37), Topps, Inc. (17, 20, 21, 24, 31, 34, 35 top right, 42 top, 43 both, 45),
Author's Collection (16), Popular Publications, Inc. (23), Pro Line/NFL Properties, Inc. (35 top left),
Petersen Publishing Co. (36), Xerographics, Inc. (38), Sprint Nextel Corp. (42 bottom), Matt Richman (48).
Cover Photo: SportsChrome

The memorabilia and artifacts pictured in this book are presented for educational and informational purposes,
and come from the collection of the author.

Editor: Mike Kennedy
Designer: Ron Jaffe
Project Management: Black Book Partners, LLC.
Special thanks to Topps, Inc.

Library of Congress Cataloging-in-Publication Data

Stewart, Mark, 1960-
  The Indianapolis Colts / by Mark Stewart.
     p. cm. -- (Team spirit)
  Includes bibliographical references and index.
  Summary: "A revised Team Spirit Football edition featuring the
Indianapolis Colts that chronicles the history and accomplishments of the
team. Includes access to the Team Spirit website which provides additional
information and photos"--Provided by publisher.
  ISBN 978-1-59953-525-8 (library edition : alk. paper) -- ISBN
978-1-60357-467-9 (ebook)
  1. Indianapolis Colts (Football team)--History--Juvenile literature. I.
Title.
  GV956.I53S85 2012
  796.332'6477252--dc23
                                          2012014483

Manufactured in the United States of America in North Mankato, Minnesota.
205N—082012

COVER PHOTO: The Colts celebrate a great defensive play during the 2010 season.

Table of Contents

ABOUT OUR GLOSSARY

In this book, there may be several words that you are reading for the first time. Some are sports words, some are new vocabulary words, and some are familiar words that are used in an unusual way. All of these words are defined on page 46. Throughout the book, sports words appear in **bold type**. Regular vocabulary words appear in ***bold italic type***.

Meet the Colts

When a football team needs to win an important game, it usually turns to its quarterback for leadership. The better the quarterback, the better a team's chances. The Indianapolis Colts have lived by this rule since the 1950s. They have been lucky to call some of football's most talented passers their own.

Of course, the Colts have not relied solely on quarterbacks to build their winning *tradition*. They look for players at every position who have great skills and big personalities. That makes the team fun to watch and hard to beat.

This book tells the story of the Colts. It is a story that begins in one city, ends in another, and covers six *decades*. During that time, two things have always been true. The Colts put players on the field who make their fans stand up and cheer. And, no fans in football have shown more love or loyalty than fans of the Colts.

Indianapolis fans love to cheer for players with passion for the game.

Glory Days

In the early days of the **National Football League (NFL)**, some teams had lots of fans, and other teams struggled. In 1950, the Baltimore Colts lost 11 of 12 games. The team soon went out of business. Football fans in Baltimore, Maryland, hoped the day would come when they could support another club.

In 1953, a local businessman named Carroll Rosenbloom brought a new team to Baltimore. He chose a familiar name: the Colts. This time, the fans came out in huge numbers. In the years that followed, they would become famous for their loyalty to the team.

Baltimore's early stars included defensive standouts Art Donovan and Gino Marchetti and a record-setting kicker named Bert Rechichar. Later in the 1950s, the Colts added talented players to their offense, including Jim Parker, Alan Ameche, Lenny Moore, and Raymond Berry. Their leader was Johnny Unitas, a skinny quarterback who was one of football's greatest passers.

In 1958, the Colts played the New York Giants for the NFL championship. It was a thrilling game that Baltimore won in **overtime**. An NFL game had never ended this way before. Millions watched it to the very end on television. They became instant NFL fans.

The Colts won the NFL championship in 1959 and again in 1968. In January of 1969, Baltimore played in its first **Super Bowl**. The Colts made it back to the Super Bowl two years later, thanks to a strong defense led by Mike Curtis and Ted Hendricks. They beat the Dallas Cowboys with a **field goal** in the final seconds.

The Colts were very good during the 1970s. Their stars included Bert Jones, Lydell Mitchell, and John Dutton. However,

LEFT: Johnny Unitas   **ABOVE**: Alan Ameche scores the winning touchdown in the 1958 NFL title game.

they did not win another championship. Team owner Robert Irsay thought a new stadium would improve the Colts' luck. When Irsay could not get funding for the project, he moved the Colts to Indianapolis, Indiana.

The people of Indiana were thrilled to have their own team. The Colts rewarded them by making a run for the Super Bowl in 1995. On the last play of the championship game of the **American Football Conference (AFC)**, Jim Harbaugh's desperate pass into the end zone fell to the ground an inch from his receiver's fingertips. Though disappointed, the Colts and their fans vowed they would return to the Super Bowl one day.

The Colts remade their team around quarterback Peyton Manning. People said Manning was born to play the position, and he was—his father had been a star passer in the 1970s. Working with a talented receiver named Marvin Harrison, Manning broke almost all of Unitas's team passing records and set many NFL marks, too.

LEFT: Peyton Manning
ABOVE: Marvin Harrison

Manning and the Colts came close to the Super Bowl several times. In 1999, they won 13 games during the regular season. Manning completed more than 100 passes to Harrison, while Edgerrin James led the rushing attack. Indianapolis fans were ready for a trip to the Super Bowl, but the Colts lost to the Tennessee Titans in the **playoffs**.

Over the next few seasons, the Colts made the **postseason** but came up short again and again. They had skilled players at almost every position—including Reggie Wayne, Dwight Freeney, Robert Mathis, Cato June, Dallas Clark, Joseph Addai, Mike Vanderjagt, Tarik Glenn, and Jeff Saturday.

Finally, in 2006, the Colts put it all together.

That season, Indianapolis finished first in the **AFC South**, and then won three tough playoff games. Manning had a great regular season and was even better in the postseason. The Colts defeated the Chicago Bears in Super Bowl XLI for their first championship since moving to Indianapolis.

In the years that followed, it seemed as if Manning would go on winning and breaking records forever. However, in 2011, a neck injury kept him out of the lineup for the entire season. Without their leader, the Colts won only two games. In 2012, the team had to make an extremely difficult choice. Unsure if Manning would fully recover, they allowed him to leave the team. They **drafted** college star Andrew Luck and began rebuilding around a new quarterback.

LEFT: Jeff Saturday
RIGHT: Reggie Wayne

Home Turf

The Colts play in a magnificent stadium on the south side of Indianapolis. The NFL liked it so much that the league hosted Super Bowl XLVI there. The stadium is also home to big events in other sports, such as college basketball's *Final Four*.

The Colts' stadium features incredible technology. A large panel of windows at one end can slide open to let fresh air into the building. The windows offer a beautiful view of downtown Indianapolis. The stadium also has a *retractable* roof that can quickly close if bad weather shows up. The Colts like the stadium for many reasons, including the fact that the crowd noise often makes it hard for opponents to hear one another.

BY THE NUMBERS

- The Colts' stadium has 63,000 seats.
- The stadium has two huge scoreboards. Each stands 97 feet high and 53 feet wide.
- When the roof is open, the opening measures 4.5 acres.

The large panel of windows can be seen at the far end of the Colts' stadium.

Dressed for Success

The team's uniform has barely changed in 50 years. It is an NFL *classic*. The team colors—blue and white—came from an old NFL team called the Dallas Texans. The horseshoe on the team's helmet was added in 1957. Fans liked to call it the "blue shoe." Before the horseshoe came along, the team's helmet was solid blue with no design. The Colts also wore a white helmet with a single blue stripe.

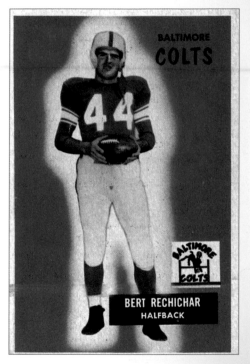

Since moving to Indianapolis, the Colts have done little to change their uniforms. Their jersey is blue with white stripes for home games and white with blue stripes for road games. Stripes have been added and taken away over the years, but the look has been the same for many decades. The team wears blue socks with its white uniforms and white socks with its blue uniforms.

LEFT: Adam Vinatieri wears the team's home uniform.
RIGHT: Bert Rechichar models the Colts uniform of the 1950s.

We Won!

To this day, many fans still call the Colts' victory over the New York Giants for the 1958 NFL championship "the greatest game ever played." The league is certainly grateful to the Colts.

Millions of people became fans of the NFL that day. They also became fans of the Colts. The Giants were the league's richest and most glamorous team. The Colts reminded fans of everyday working people.

Johnny Unitas guided Baltimore to a pair of touchdowns in the first half, including a scoring pass to Raymond Berry. The Giants came back in the second half to take a 17–14 lead. With two minutes left, Unitas got the ball back and went to work. He completed one pass after another to drive the Colts down the field. Kicker

EARL MORRALL

COLTS
QUARTERBACK • A.F.C.

LEFT: Raymond Berry signed this photo, which shows him in the 1950s.
RIGHT: Earl Morrall quarterbacked the 1968 team.

Steve Myhra then booted a field goal to tie the score. For the first time in NFL history, a game went into overtime.

The extra period was called "sudden death," because the game would end as soon as one team scored. The pressure was incredible. The Giants got the ball first, and the Colts stopped them. When Baltimore got the ball, Unitas picked apart the New York defense again. Finally, he handed the ball to Alan Ameche, who smashed into the end zone for six points and a 23–17 victory. The thrilling victory energized *professional* football.

One year later, the Colts and Giants met again for the championship. The game was very close until the fourth quarter. Unitas took over, and Baltimore won 31–16.

The Colts claimed their third NFL championship in 1968. They beat the Cleveland Browns, 34–0. Unitas was injured, but his replacement, Earl Morrall, provided steady leadership. Meanwhile, running back Tom Matte had a great game and scored three touchdowns.

The Colts won their fourth NFL championship two years later in Super Bowl V. They defeated the Dallas Cowboys, 16–13. It was a rough game that was *dominated* by the defenses, and it had a very exciting finish. Mike Curtis **intercepted** a Dallas pass with time running out, and Jim O'Brien booted a 32-yard field goal for the victory.

The next time the Colts played in the Super Bowl was 2006. This time, they represented the city of Indianapolis. They had won their first nine games with a high-powered offense led by

Peyton Manning. He had two great receivers in Marvin Harrison and Reggie Wayne. Joseph Addai was the team's top runner. Indianapolis survived several injuries to its defense and rolled into Super Bowl XLI against the Chicago Bears.

The game started terribly for the Colts when Devin Hester ran back the opening kickoff for a touchdown. Chicago scored again later in the first quarter, but the Colts began to toughen up on defense. They forced five **turnovers** and allowed just three more points the rest of the game.

With his receivers **double-covered**, Manning turned to his running backs. He completed 10 passes to Addai, and Dominic Rhodes ran for more than 100 yards. With the Colts leading in the fourth quarter, Kevin Hayden intercepted a pass and returned it 56 yards for a touchdown. The final score was 29–16, and Manning was named the game's **Most Valuable Player (MVP)**.

LEFT: Jim O'Brien jumps for joy after his winning kick.
ABOVE: Peyton Manning celebrates a touchdown pass.

Go-To Guys

To be a true star in the NFL, you need more than fast feet and a big body. You have to be a "go-to guy"—someone the coach wants on the field at the end of a big game. Colts fans have had a lot to cheer about over the years, including these great stars …

THE PIONEERS

GINO
MARCHETTI
BALTIMORE COLTS
DEFENSIVE END

GINO MARCHETTI   Defensive End

- Born: 1/2/1927
- Played for Team: 1953 to 1964 & 1966

Gino Marchetti invented many of the pass-rushing moves you see today in NFL games. He often combined several moves to **sack** the quarterback.

ALAN AMECHE   Running Back

- Born: 3/1/1933   • Died: 8/8/1988   • Played for Team: 1955 to 1960

Alan Ameche's nickname was "The Horse" because he ran so hard. He gained 410 yards in his first three games as an NFL **rookie**. That set a record that stood for 50 years. Ameche was voted to the **Pro Bowl** four years in a row.

JOHNNY UNITAS   Quarterback

• BORN: 5/7/1933   • DIED: 9/11/2002   • PLAYED FOR TEAM: 1956 TO 1972

Johnny Unitas was one of the best quarterbacks in history. Unitas had a strong and accurate arm, and he played his best in the final minutes of close games. He made the **Hall of Fame** in 1979.

RAYMOND BERRY   Receiver

• BORN: 2/27/1933   • PLAYED FOR TEAM: 1955 TO 1967

Raymond Berry was a great receiver. He ran his patterns to perfection and almost never dropped a ball. Johnny Unitas could throw a pass to an empty spot on the field, confident that Berry would be there to catch it when it came down.

JIM PARKER   Offensive Lineman

• BORN: 4/3/1934   • DIED: 7/18/2005
• PLAYED FOR TEAM: 1957 TO 1967

Jim Parker was the NFL's best blocker. He was voted **All-Pro** as a tackle and then All-Pro when he moved over to play guard.

LENNY MOORE   Running Back/Receiver

• BORN: 11/25/1933   • PLAYED FOR TEAM: 1956 TO 1967

Lenny Moore was a speedy and talented runner and receiver. For many years, he was the most dangerous player in the NFL. Moore could score at any time, on any play.

LENNY MOORE
BALTIMORE COLTS   HALFBACK

LEFT: Gino Marchetti
RIGHT: Lenny Moore

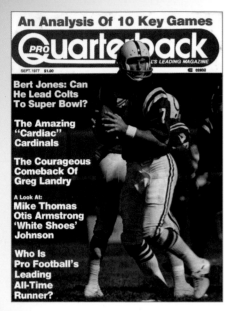

BERT JONES · Quarterback

• BORN: 9/7/1951 • PLAYED FOR TEAM: 1973 TO 1981

Bert Jones grew up playing catch with an NFL receiver—his father, Dub Jones. It only made sense that he became an NFL quarterback. Jones was named the league MVP in 1976.

ERIC DICKERSON · Running Back

• BORN: 9/2/1960 • PLAYED FOR TEAM: 1987 TO 1991

Eric Dickerson was a powerful runner who came to the Colts in a trade on Halloween night in 1987. He helped them reach the playoffs a few months later. In 1988, Dickerson led the NFL in rushing with 1,659 yards.

MARSHALL FAULK · Running Back

• BORN: 2/26/1973 • PLAYED FOR TEAM: 1994 TO 1998

Marshall Faulk followed the Colts' tradition of do-it-all running backs. He gained 1,000 rushing yards in four of his five seasons with Indianapolis and caught nearly 300 passes as a Colt.

MARVIN HARRISON · Receiver

• BORN: 8/25/1972 • PLAYED FOR TEAM: 1996 TO 2008

Marvin Harrison caught more than 1,000 passes for the Colts. He did his job quietly and became a respected leader for the team. When Harrison retired, he was second on the NFL's all-time list for pass receptions.

PEYTON MANNING   Quarterback

- BORN: 3/24/1976   • PLAYED FOR TEAM: 1998 TO 2011

Peyton Manning was the heart and soul of the Colts for more than a decade. He threw for more than 50,000 yards and nearly 400 touchdowns during that time. Manning was voted All-Pro five times and the NFL MVP four times. He was also the MVP of Super Bowl XLI.

REGGIE WAYNE   Receiver

- BORN: 11/17/1978   • FIRST YEAR WITH TEAM: 2001

After Marvin Harrison retired, Reggie Wayne became Peyton Manning's most trusted receiver. He caught more than 100 passes three times in a four-year span. In 2007, Wayne led the NFL with 1,510 receiving yards.

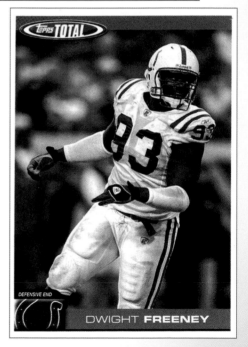

DWIGHT FREENEY   Defensive End

- BORN: 1/4/1978   • FIRST YEAR WITH TEAM: 2002

At just a shade over 6´ 1″, Dwight Freeney was short for a defensive end. But he put up big numbers from his very first year with the Colts. Freeney became one of the team's greatest pass-rushers and tacklers.

LEFT: Bert Jones
RIGHT: Dwight Freeney

Calling the Shots

Coaching the Colts has been one of the top jobs in sports for more than 50 years. Weeb Ewbank helped make it that way. He took over the Colts in their second season. Critics laughed when Ewbank predicted that the team would win a championship within four years. But Ewbank was confident, and the Colts proved him right in 1958.

In 1963, Don Shula replaced Ewbank. The Colts finished first or second six years in a row under Shula and lost only 23 games in the seven years he coached the team. In 1968, he led the Colts to a 13–1 record and the NFL title.

Another coach who had great success with the Colts was Ted Marchibroda. He guided the team in the 1970s and again in the 1990s. Under Marchibroda, the team made the playoffs in Baltimore and again after the move to Indianapolis.

The Colts searched hard for a coach who could match Marchibroda's success. The man who made that happen was Tony Dungy. At first, fans were unhappy with the way Dungy ran the team. They said he did not prepare the Colts well for the playoffs. In 2006, Dungy made small changes to the defense that had big results in the postseason. The Colts went on to win Super Bowl XLI.

In 2009, Dungy handed the team over to one of his most trusted assistant coaches, Jim Caldwell. He had worked with Peyton Manning for many years. In his first season, Caldwell led Indianapolis to an amazing 14–2 record and a return trip to the Super Bowl!

One Great Day

Football on Thanksgiving is an NFL tradition. Every year since 1930, the Detroit Lions have hosted a "Turkey Day" game. There is a lot of pressure to win on Thanksgiving. Millions of fans plan their holiday meal around this game. No one wants to look bad in front of so many people.

In 2004, the Colts traveled to Detroit—and made the Lions look like turkeys. Indianapolis had one of the league's most dangerous offenses. Peyton Manning was having the best year of his career. He would finish the season passing for 4,557 yards and 49 touchdowns.

Detroit decided the best way to beat the Colts was to have two defenders shadow receiver Marvin Harrison all day long.

LEFT: Peyton Manning
RIGHT: Marvin Harrison

Manning responded by relying more on his other receivers, including Brandon Stokely. The strategy worked. Manning found Stokely in the end zone three times in a row for touchdown passes.

The Lions had seen enough. They began to pay closer attention to Stokely. Manning crossed them up by going back to Harrison. Three more times he threw touchdown passes—each one to Harrison.

The Lions, meanwhile, could not get into the end zone against the Indianapolis defense. The Colts had three sacks on the day and intercepted a pass. Detroit managed just three field goals. The Colts won easily, 41–9. Manning's six touchdown passes were one short of the record for a single game. The Lions and their fans were happy to see him and the Colts leave town.

Legend Has It

Who were the greatest pass-rushers in team history?

LEGEND HAS IT that the "Sack Pack" was. The Colts have had many players who were great at putting pressure on the quarterback, including Gino Marchetti, Bubba Smith, and Dwight Freeney. But the team's 1975 defensive line—Fred Cook, John Dutton, Mike Barnes, and Joe Ehrmann—earned their nickname by setting a team record with 59 sacks.

ABOVE: Fred Cook, John Dutton, Mike Barnes, and Joe Ehrmann were Baltimore's Sack Pack   RIGHT: Peyton Manning

LEGEND HAS IT that Peyton Manning was. Most fans thought that Art Donovan was the team's king of comedy. After all, he wrote a best-selling book of funny football stories. Many fans also got a kick out of Bubba Smith. He was an actor who appeared in funny movies and commercials. But Manning topped them both when he hosted *Saturday Night Live* in 2007. He

filmed two fake commercials and did a locker room dance that had the audience in tears.

Who was the Colts' top touchdown-maker?

LEGEND HAS IT that Lenny Moore was. Johnny Unitas set a record by throwing touchdown passes in 47 games in a row. But Moore's streak may be even more impressive. From 1963 to 1965, he scored at least one touchdown in 18 straight games. Some came on passes from Unitas, but most were scored on running plays. Moore's NFL record stood for 40 seasons.

W hat happens when a team runs out of quarterbacks? The Colts found out in 1965 after Johnny Unitas and Gary Cuozzo were struck down by injuries in the final month of the season. The Colts had won enough games by that point to compete for a playoff spot. But what was coach Don Shula going to do about a quarterback? He had no choice but to turn to Tom Matte, who played running back for the team.

The Colts faced the Los Angeles Rams in the final game of the year needing a victory to make the postseason. The Rams had a great defense. Their pass rushers were nicknamed the "Fearsome Foursome." Matte wasn't worried. He led the Colts to a 20–17 victory.

The Colts and the Green Bay Packers were now tied for first place in the **Western Conference**. They met to decide who would move on to the **NFL Championship Game**. The contest was tense from the opening kickoff. Matte wrote Baltimore's passing plays down on his wristband. In the huddle, he read the play he wanted to run to his teammates. That wristband is now in the Hall of Fame.

Neither team could gain an
advantage. The score was tied after
60 minutes. In overtime, the Packers
kicked a field goal for a 13–10 victory.
To this day, Colts fans believe that
kick was wide.

But Baltimore's season wasn't
over. The Colts faced the Dallas
Cowboys in a special game called
the Playoff Bowl. Matte was terrific.
He threw two touchdown passes to
Jimmy Orr. Matte's replacement at
running back, Jerry Hill, also chipped in with two touchdowns. The
Colts won easily, 35–3.

Afterwards, Shula was asked what he thought about his new
passing star. "Now we'll probably have to keep a Matte offense in our
playbook!" he joked.

Team Spirit

Colts fans love their team—no matter where they live. In fact, they may be the most loyal fans in the NFL. When the Colts played in Baltimore, the team sold out Memorial Stadium 51 times in a row from 1964 to 1970. At that time, this was the longest "sellout streak" in NFL history.

Fans of the Colts know a lot about heartbreak. Baltimore fans were shocked when the Colts moved to Indianapolis in 1984. Thousands continued to root for them until Baltimore got a new NFL team, the Ravens, in 1996.

When the people of Indianapolis learned that the Colts were coming to town, they were overjoyed. One of the toughest days was when Peyton Manning left the team. But true to form, the fans stuck with the Colts. When Indianapolis drafted Andrew Luck in 2012, they began dreaming of their next Super Bowl championship.

LEFT: The loyalty of Indianapolis fans knows no limit.
ABOVE: This pin was sold at Memorial Stadium in the 1970s.

Timeline

n this timeline, each Super Bowl is listed under the year it was played. Remember that the Super Bowl is held early in the year and is actually part of the previous season. For example, Super Bowl XLVI was played on February 5, 2012, but it was the championship of the 2011 NFL season.

1969
The Colts reach the Super Bowl for the first time.

1953
The Colts join the NFL.

1955
Alan Ameche leads the NFL in rushing.

1958
The Colts win their first NFL championship.

1971
The Colts win Super Bowl V.

Art Donovan

TACKLE-COLTS

Art Donovan was a leader of the 1958 Colts.

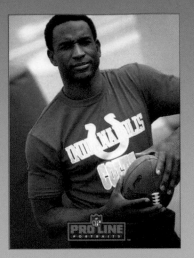

Eric
Dickerson

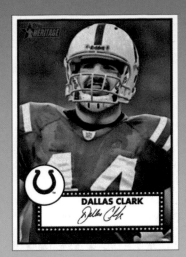

Dallas
Clark

1988
Eric Dickerson leads
the league in rushing.

2002
Marvin Harrison sets
an NFL record with
143 receptions.

2009
Dallas Clark is
named All-Pro.

1984
The Colts move
to Indianapolis.

2006
The Colts win their
second Super Bowl.

2012
The Colts take Andrew
Luck first in the draft.

Joseph Addai
starred for the
2006 champs.

Fun Facts

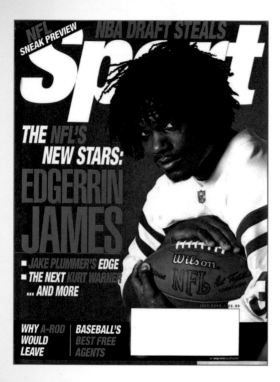

FAST START

Edgerrin James ran for more than 1,500 yards four times in his first seven seasons. Only three other players in history had done that.

EIGHT IS GREAT

For eight seasons from 1999 to 2006, Marvin Harrison had at least 1,000 yards and 10 touchdown catches every season. No receiver had ever done that before.

FIRST TIME FOR EVERYTHING

In a 1953 game against the Chicago Bears, Bert Rechichar set an NFL record by kicking a 56-yard field goal. It was the first field goal he had ever attempted in his life!

ABOVE: Edgerrin James   **RIGHT**: Buddy Young

YOUNG LOVE

Claude "Buddy" Young was the smallest man in football when he played for the Colts—he stood just 5′ 4″. After joining the team in 1953, he was voted Baltimore's most popular player.

BURGER KING

In the 1970s, one of the most popular fast food restaurants in the United States was called Gino's. It was started by Hall of Famer Gino Marchetti.

LONG TIME COMING

In 2005, safety Bob Sanders was picked to play in the Pro Bowl. The last time the Colts had sent a defensive back to the league's annual all-star game was 1971, when Rick Volk and Jerry Logan represented the team.

BIGGER IS BETTER

Art Donovan was a big man who weighed 300 pounds. Everyone called him "Fatso," but Donovan got the last laugh. He was the first member of the Colts to make it to the Hall of Fame.

Talking Football

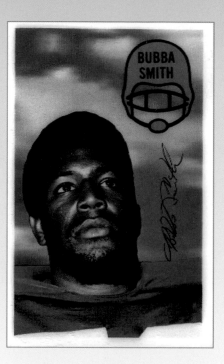

"I just tackle the whole **backfield** and throw guys out until I come to the one with the ball."

▶ **Bubba Smith,** *on his defensive strategy*

"There's an old saying that goes, 'Lead by example and when necessary use words.' That's what Marvin did. He rarely used words."

▶ **Jim Caldwell,** *on Marvin Harrison's quiet leadership*

"I never had any idea when I was playing or retired that fans would still be in my life this many years later."

▶ **Raymond Berry,** *on his popularity with Colts fans*

" I believe if I stay tall and run up high, I can see better."

▶ **Eric Dickerson,** *on his unusual upright running style*

"The players I played with and the coaches I had—they are directly responsible for my being here. I want you all to remember that. I always will."

▶ *Johnny Unitas, on how he became a Hall of Famer*

"I've never left the field saying, 'I could've done more to get ready,' and that gives me peace of mind."

▶ *Peyton Manning, on why he spent so much time preparing for each game*

"A guy can be lying on the ground and you touch him and you get a sack, or a guy runs out of bounds and you get one. You never know how it's going to happen."

▶ *Dwight Freeney, on why he never gives up when trying for a sack*

"Don't forget about studying. If playing in the NFL is your Plan A, then make sure you have a Plan B. You have to have options."

▶ *Lydell Mitchell, on the importance of education*

LEFT: Bubba Smith
ABOVE: Johnny Unitas

Great Debates

People who root for the Colts love to compare their favorite moments, teams, and players. Some debates have been going on for years! How would you settle these classic football arguments?

Peyton Manning was the Colts' greatest passer ....

... because he holds almost every team record for quarterbacks. Manning (   ) set career records with 4,682 completions for 54,828 yards and 399 touchdowns. He also set single-game records for the most completions (40), passing yards (472), and touchdowns (6). Manning was a great leader. He led the Colts to the Super Bowl twice and won the championship once.

Numbers don't tell the whole story. Johnny Unitas was the best ...

... because he was truly unstoppable. From 1956 to 1960, Unitas threw at least one touchdown pass in 47 games in a row. He won two MVP trophies during that time and two more during the 1960s. In 1958 and 1959, Unitas led the Colts to a pair of NFL championships. Eleven years later, he passed the Colts to victory in Super Bowl V. No one has ever been that good for that long.

... because their talent and toughness were off the charts. Johnny Unitas was just one of several superstars on the Colts. Five of his teammates were also elected to the Hall of Fame! The Colts proved how great they were in 1958 with a comeback victory in the NFL title game. One year later, they won another championship.

Not so fast. The 2006 Colts would blow away the 1958 team ...

... because they had a huge advantage in speed and strength. Who on the 1958 Colts would cover Reggie Wayne (RIGHT) and Marvin Harrison? And what about Dallas Clark? He was a great tight end. Manning would pick the Baltimore defense apart. Speaking of defense, the 2006 Colts were tough. Would Raymond Berry catch balls against Bob Sanders? Would Jim Parker be able to handle Dwight Freeney? It would be a great game, but Manning and his teammates would definitely win.

For the Record

The great Colts teams and players have left their marks on the record books. These are the "best of the best" ...

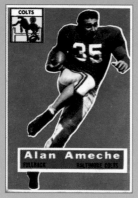

Alan Ameche

Marshall Faulk

COLTS AWARD WINNERS

WINNER	AWARD	YEAR
Alan Ameche	Rookie of the Year	1955
Lenny Moore	Rookie of the Year	1956
Johnny Unitas	Most Valuable Player	1957
Weeb Ewbank	Coach of the Year	1958
Johnny Unitas	Most Valuable Player	1964
Don Shula	Coach of the Year	1964
Johnny Unitas	Most Valuable Player	1967
Earl Morrall	Most Valuable Player	1968
Don Shula	Coach of the Year	1968
Ted Marchibroda	Coach of the Year	1975
Bert Jones	Most Valuable Player	1976
Vernon Maxwell	Defensive Rookie of the Year	1983
Duane Bickett	Defensive Rookie of the Year	1985
Marshall Faulk	Offensive Rookie of the Year	1994
Edgerrin James	Offensive Rookie of the Year	1999
Peyton Manning	co-Most Valuable Player	2003
Peyton Manning	Most Valuable Player	2004
Peyton Manning	Super Bowl XLI MVP	2006
Bob Sanders	Defensive Player of the Year	2007
Peyton Manning	Most Valuable Player	2008
Peyton Manning	Most Valuable Player	2009

COLTS ACHIEVEMENTS

ACHIEVEMENT	YEAR
Western Conference Champions	1958
NFL Champions	1958
Western Conference Champions	1959
NFL Champions	1959
Western Conference Champions	1964
Coastal Division Champions	1968
NFL Champions	1968
AFC East Champions	1970
AFC Champions	1970
Super Bowl V Champions	1970*
AFC East Champions	1975
AFC East Champions	1976
AFC East Champions	1977
AFC East Champions	1987
AFC East Champions	1999
AFC South Champions	2003
AFC South Champions	2004
AFC South Champions	2005
Super Bowl XLI Champions	2006*
AFC South Champions	2006
AFC South Champions	2007
AFC South Champions	2009
AFC South Champions	2010

*Super Bowls are played early the following year, but the game
is counted as the championship of this season.*

JIMMY ORR
BALTIMORE COLTS   FLANKER

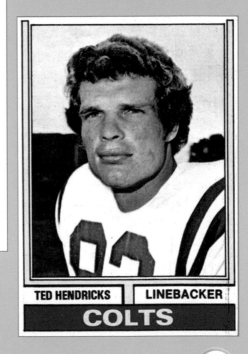

TED HENDRICKS   LINEBACKER
COLTS

TOP: Jimmy Orr was a star for the Baltimore teams of the 1960s.
RIGHT: Ted Hendricks played for the Colts in Super Bowl III.

Pinpoints

The history of a football team is made up of many smaller stories. These stories take place all over the map—not just in the city a team calls "home." Match the pushpins on these maps to the **Team Facts**, and you will begin to see the story of the Colts unfold!

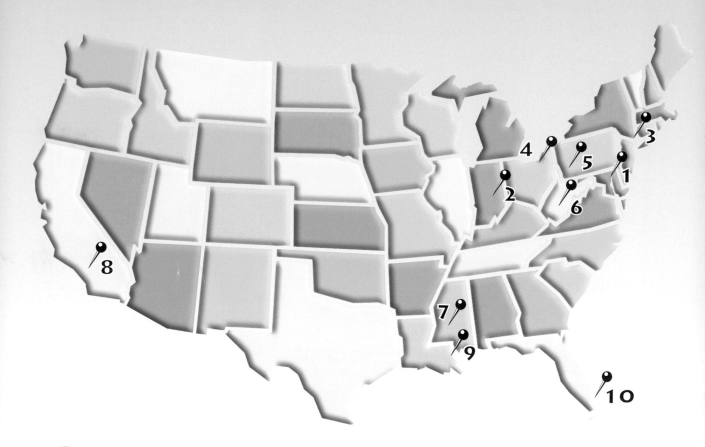

1 Baltimore, Maryland—*The team played here from 1953 to 1983.*

2 Indianapolis, Indiana—*The team has played here since 1984.*

3 Bronx, New York—*Art Donovan was born here.*

4 Cleveland, Ohio—*The Colts won the 1968 NFL championship here.*

5 Pittsburgh, Pennsylvania—*Johnny Unitas was born here.*

6 Smithers, West Virginia—*Gino Marchetti was born here.*

7 Jackson, Mississippi—*Tony Dungy was born here.*

8 Riverside, California—*Cato June was born here.*

9 New Orleans, Louisiana—*Peyton Manning was born here.*

10 Miami, Florida—*The Colts won Super Bowl XLI here.*

11 Oakville, Ontario, Canada—*Mike Vanderjagt was born here*

12 Guatemala City, Guatemala—*Ted Hendricks was born here.*

JOHNNY UNITAS
QUARTERBACK   BALTIMORE COLTS

Johnny Unitas

Glossary

🧠 **AFC SOUTH**—A division for teams that play in the southern part of the country.

🧠 **ALL-PRO**—An honor given to the best players at their positions at the end of each season.

🧠 **AMERICAN FOOTBALL CONFERENCE (AFC)**—One of two groups of teams that make up the NFL.

🧠 **BACKFIELD**—The players who line up behind the line of scrimmage. On offense, the quarterback and running backs are in the backfield.

🔗 *CLASSIC*—Popular for a long time.

🔗 *DECADES*—Periods of 10 years; also specific periods, such as the 1950s.

🔗 *DOMINATED*—Completely controlled.

🧠 **DOUBLE-COVERED**—Guarded by two defenders.

🧠 **DRAFTED**—Chosen from a group of the best college players. The NFL draft is held each spring.

🧠 **FIELD GOAL**—A goal from the field, kicked over the crossbar and between the goal posts. A field goal is worth three points.

🔗 *FINAL FOUR*—The term used for the last two rounds of the nation's official college basketball championship tournament.

🧠 **HALL OF FAME**—The museum in Canton, Ohio, where football's greatest players are honored. A player voted into the Hall of Fame is sometimes called a "Hall of Famer."

🧠 **INTERCEPTED**—Caught in the air by a defensive player.

🧠 **MOST VALUABLE PLAYER (MVP)**—The award given each year to the league's best player; also given to the best player in the Super Bowl and Pro Bowl.

🧠 **NATIONAL FOOTBALL LEAGUE (NFL)**—The league that started in 1920 and is still operating today.

🧠 **NFL CHAMPIONSHIP GAME**—The game played to decide the winner of the league each year from 1933 to 1969.

🧠 **OVERTIME**—The extra period played when a game is tied after 60 minutes.

🧠 **PLAYOFFS**—The games played after the regular season to determine which teams play in the Super Bowl.

🧠 **POSTSEASON**—Another term for playoffs.

🧠 **PRO BOWL**—The NFL's all-star game, played after the regular season.

🔗 *PROFESSIONAL*—Paid to play.

🔗 *RETRACTABLE*—Able to be pulled back.

🧠 **ROOKIE**—A player in his first season.

🧠 **SACK**—Tackle of the quarterback behind the line of scrimmage.

🧠 **SUPER BOWL**—The championship of the NFL, played between the winners of the National Football Conference and American Football Conference.

🔗 *TRADITION*—A belief or custom that is handed down from generation to generation.

🧠 **TURNOVERS**—Fumbles or interceptions that give possession of the ball to the opposing team.

🧠 **WESTERN CONFERENCE**—A group of teams that play in the western part of the country.

OVERTIME

TEAM SPIRIT introduces a great way to stay up to date with your team! Visit our **OVERTIME** link and get connected to the latest and greatest updates. **OVERTIME** serves as a young reader's ticket to an exclusive web page—with more stories, fun facts, team records, and photos of the Colts. Content is updated during and after each season. The **OVERTIME** feature also enables readers to send comments and letters to the author! Log onto:

www.norwoodhousepress.com/library.aspx

and click on the tab: **TEAM SPIRIT** to access **OVERTIME**.

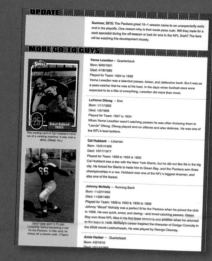

Read all the books in the series to learn more about professional sports. For a complete listing of the baseball, basketball, football, and hockey teams in the **TEAM SPIRIT** series, visit our website at:

www.norwoodhousepress.com/library.aspx

On the Road

THE INDIANAPOLIS COLTS
100 South Capitol Avenue
Indianapolis, Indiana 46225
317-297-2658
www.colts.com

THE PRO FOOTBALL HALL OF FAME
2121 George Halas Drive NW
Canton, Ohio 44708
330-456-8207
www.profootballhof.com

On the Bookshelf

To learn more about the sport of football, look for these books at your library or bookstore:

* Frederick, Shane. *The Best of Everything Football Book.* North Mankato, Minnesota: Capstone Press, 2011.

* Jacobs, Greg. *The Everything Kids' Football Book: The All-Time Greats, Legendary Teams, Today's Superstars—And Tips on Playing Like a Pro.* Avon, Massachusetts: Adams Media Corporation, 2010.

* Editors of *Sports Illustrated for Kids. 1st and 10: Top 10 Lists of Everything in Football.* New York, New York: Sports Illustrated Books, 2011.

Index

About the Author

MARK STEWART has written more than 50 books on football and over 150 sports books for kids. He grew up in New York City during the 1960s rooting for the Giants and Jets, and was lucky enough to meet players from both teams. Mark comes from a family of writers. His grandfather was Sunday Editor of *The New York Times,* and his mother was Articles Editor of *Ladies' Home Journal* and *McCall's.* Mark has profiled hundreds of athletes over the past 25 years. He has also written several books about his native New York and New Jersey, his home today. Mark is a graduate of Duke University, with a degree in history. He lives and works in a home overlooking Sandy Hook, New Jersey. You can contact Mark through the Norwood House Press website.